BORDERS AND MOTIFS
Cross Stitch Patterns

*Transform ordinary
into extraordinary
with every stitched border.*

Sakura Mai

General instructions

Before you start:

Get creative with this large book full of cross-stitch border designs. They're perfect for adding a personal touch to napkins, making pillows more special, giving quotes an extra charm, crafting unique bookmarks, and much more. All designs are presented in full colors with symbols, and there's a preview of the original artwork beside each one, allowing you to see what it will look like. Additionally, a color key table for DMC floss is included.

Fabric

Counted cross stitch is executed on even-weave fabrics, specifically manufactured for counted-thread embroidery. These fabrics are woven with the same number of vertical and horizontal threads per inch, determining the size of the finished design.

Aida fabric is fantastic for cross-stitch as it is an even weave. It's also a favorite among beginning stitchers because its weave forms distinctive squares in the fabric, making it easy to place stitches and allowing you to create straight lines while you stitch. Aida is measured by «count», 14 count Aida has 14 squares per inch, and 18 count has 18 squares per inch. The more squares per inch, the smaller the stitches and overall pattern will be.

Number of strands

The number of strands used varies depending on the fabric. Generally, the rule to follow for cross-stitching is three strands on Aida 11, two strands on Aida 14, one or two strands on Aida 18 (depending on the desired thickness of stitches), and one strand on Hardanger 22.
For backstitching, use one strand on all fabrics.

Preparing the fabric

Cut the fabric at least 3 inches larger on each side than the finished design size to ensure enough space for the desired assembly. To prevent fraying, whipstitch, machine-zigzag, or apply masking tape along the raw edges.

Cleaning the finished design

When you are finished, you can give your fabric a gentle hand wash in cold water with mild soap. Rinse well and roll it in a towel to remove excess water. Don't wring it, instead, place it face down on a dry towel and iron on a warm setting until the fabric is dry.

Cross stitch

• Danish method

Consist of doing one half of the stitch in one direction, then coming back to do the other half of the stitch. Stitches are done in a row or, if necessary, one at a time in an area.

This method is ideal for working in big blocks of color, as you can go in one direction, then back, ending up at the beginning of the next row or column. This method uses fewer threads and leaves the back of your work neat.

<u>Steps:</u>

1. Insert the needle up between interlacing threads at A.
2. Go down at B, the opening diagonally across from A.
3. Come up at C and go down at D, etc.
4. To complete the top stitches creating an "X", come up at E and go down at B, come up at C and go down at F, etc. All top stitches should be in the same direction.

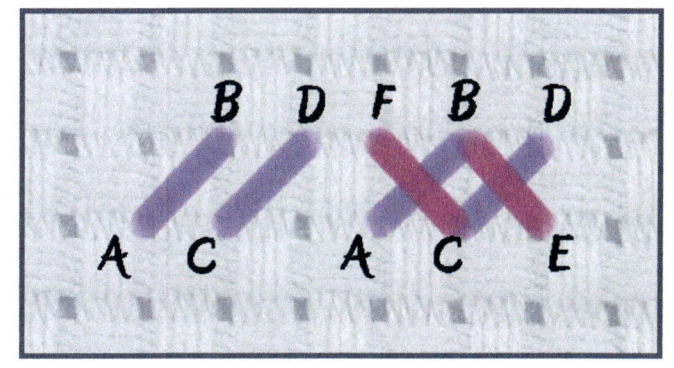

- ### English method

Consists of completing each cross at once, it's often the easier method to use when dealing with randomly scattered stitches of one color across your pattern.

Steps:
1. Insert the needle up between interlacing threads at A.
2. Go down at B, the opening diagonally across from A.
3. Come up at C and go down at D to complete a full "X".
4. To continue the second "X", come up at E and go down at D, come up at B and go down at F, etc.

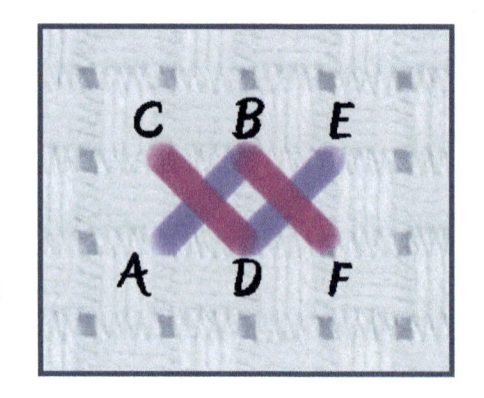

There is no right or wrong way to do cross-stitch. It's all about experimenting with both methods, the more you stitch, the more you will discover your own rhythm and see which one works best for you most of the time.

Backstitch

Backstitching is usually used for intricate and detailed designs. Though it is not required by the patterns in this book, you can still add it when you feel it's needed.

Steps:
5. Insert the needle up between interlacing threads at A.
6. Go down at B, one opening to the right.
7. Come up at C.
8. Go down at A, one opening to the right.

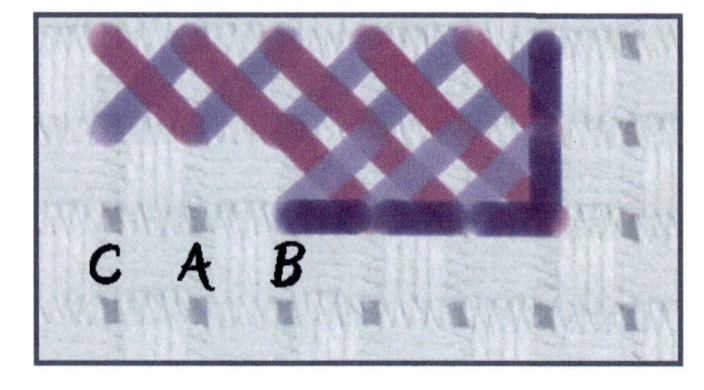

How to adjust the patterns to be bigger or smaller?

The simplest method is to use the pattern as is, but you need to alter the size or count number of your Aida cloth. If you would like your design to be larger, use a smaller count, such as 6, 8, or 11-count Aida cloth, which has larger squares (fewer squares per inch) and can make your finished design larger. This method will work if you prefer to reduce your pattern size too, just use a lower count Aida like 18 or 24, and your finished design will come out smaller.

How to figure out how much bigger (or smaller) it will be?

The general rule is simple! Here's the math:
Stitch count of design / Aida cloth count = finished size in inches
Note that you will have to make 2 calculations: 1 for the length and 1 for the width.
Example: We have 28 squares in the width, and let's say we decide to use 14 squares of Aida fabric:
28 stitches / 14 count Aida = 2 inches

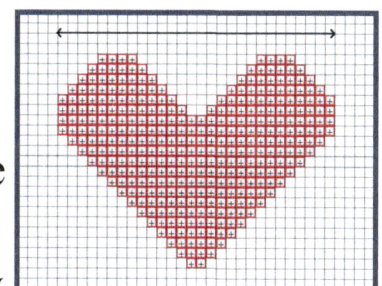

Tips

- Your thread count and the number of strands you use can change your pattern's outcome. I suggest using three strands instead of two if you are looking for more coverage.
- Use beads, sequins, charms, buttons, and other embellishments to change the overall style of a finished piece. Match elements to the style you are going for, and take care not to overdo it. Usually, only one of these elements is best. These elements can also be good fillers for negative space on your fabric background.
- Feel free to experiment with different colors for these patterns and customize them according to your liking. For color combination ideas, you might want to check out the book 'Four Seasons Embroidery Color Palettes: 100 Embroidery Floss Color Charts' at https://www.amazon.com/dp/B0C68GRB8W

Legend:
- ♥ DMC-347 salmon - vy dk
- ▲ DMC-924 gray green - vy dk
- ✹ DMC-988 forest green - md

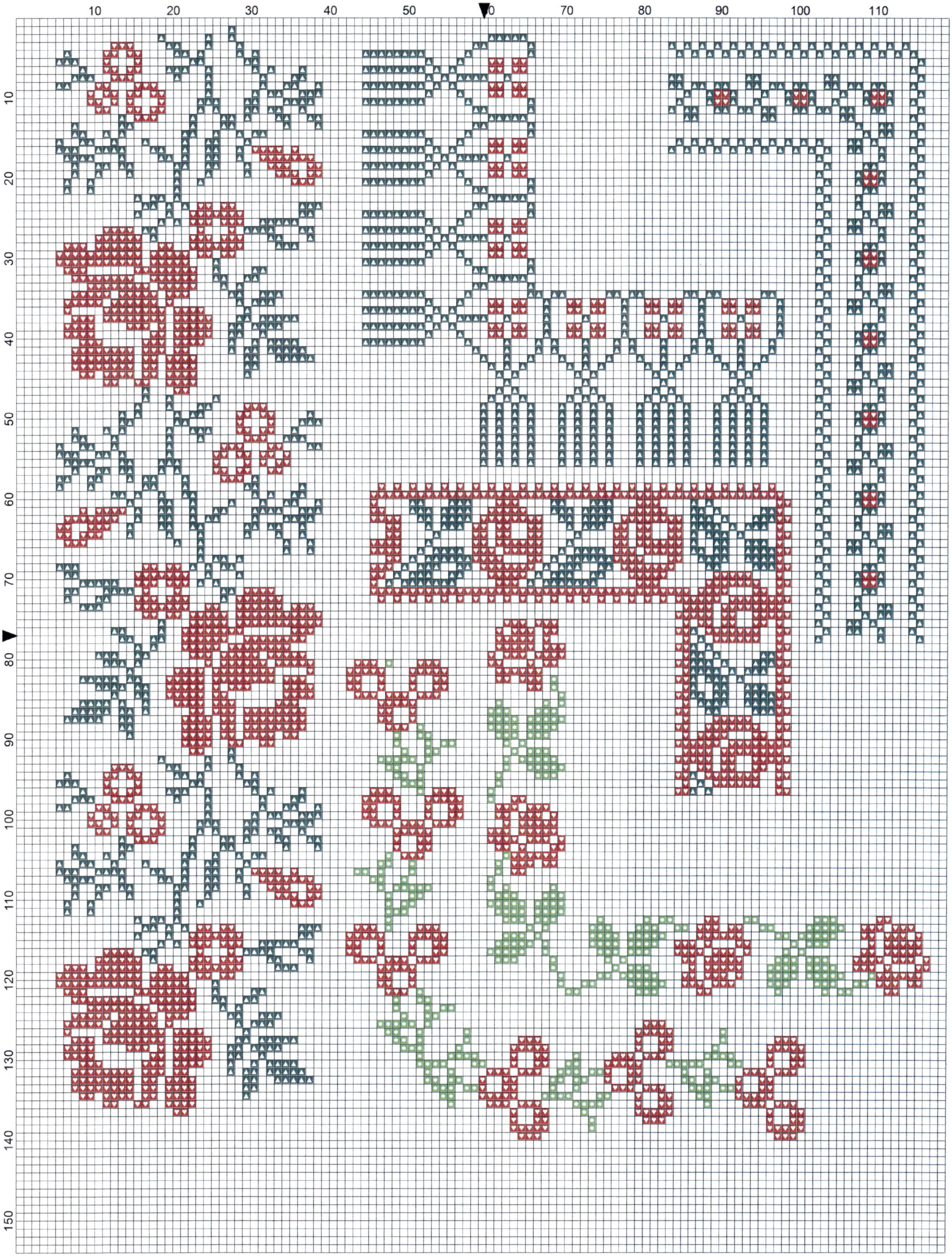

Legend:
- ♥ DMC-347 salmon - vy dk
- ✚ DMC-606 burnt orange-red
- ♦ DMC-817 coral red - vy dk
- ◐ DMC-905 parrot green - dk
- ♠ DMC-906 parrot green - md
- ▲ DMC-988 forest green - md
- ✳ DMC-3787 brown gray - dk

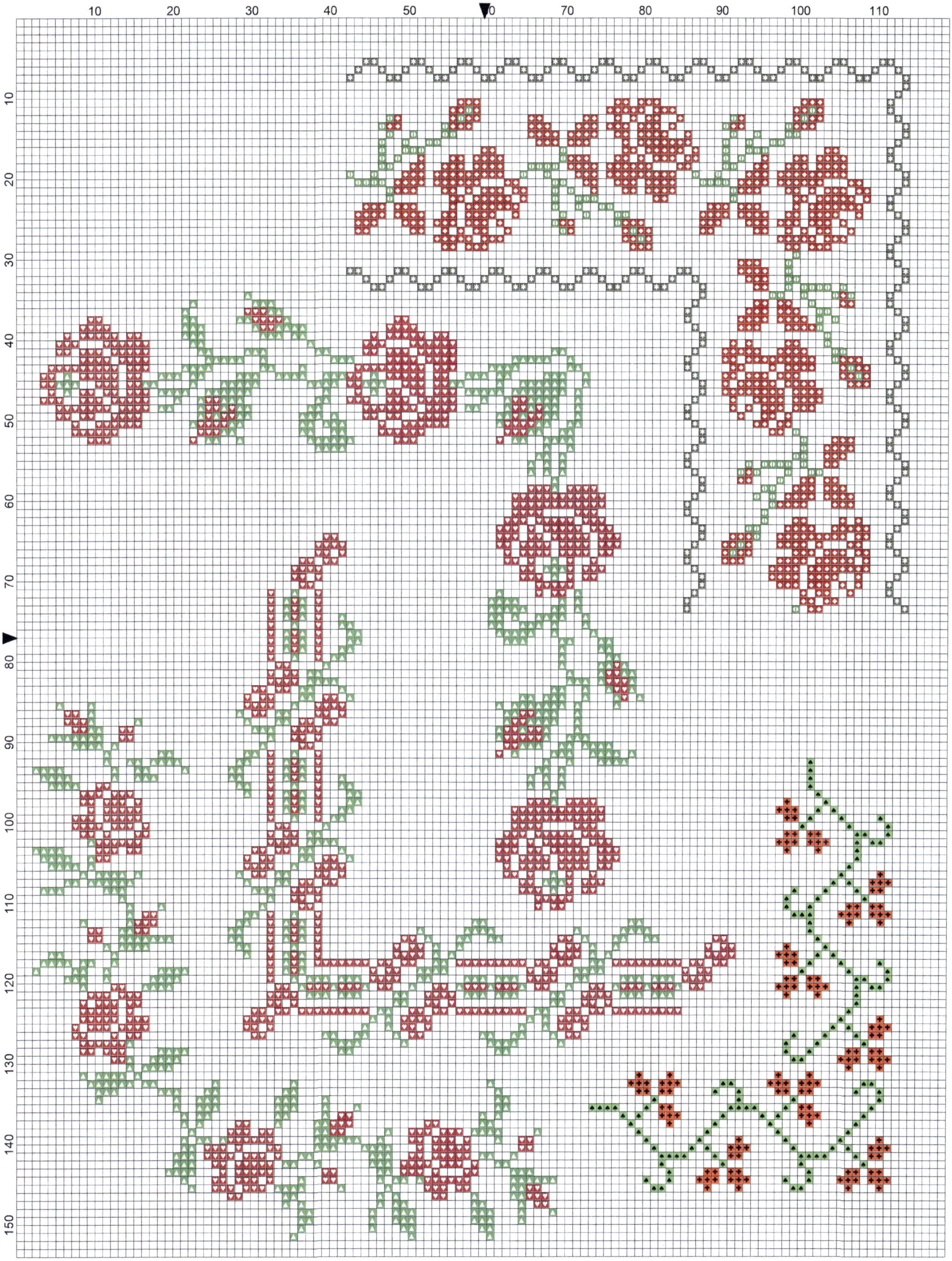
10
20
30
40
50
60
70
80
90
100
110
120
130
140
150

Legend:
- ◆ DMC-347 salmon - vy dk
- ♥ DMC-817 coral red - vy dk
- ★ DMC-905 parrot green - dk
- ■ DMC-924 gray green - vy dk
- ✖ DMC-3787 brown gray - dk

10 20 30 40 50 60 70 80 90 100 110
10 20 30 40 50 60 70 80 90 100 110 120 130 140 150

Legend:

Symbol	Color	DMC	Name
✖		DMC-21	alizarin - lt
●		DMC-28	eggplant - md lt
◆		DMC-307	lemon
✚		DMC-472	avocado green - ul lt
━		DMC-598	turquoise - lt
♥		DMC-600	cranberry - vy dk
▲		DMC-604	cranberry - lt
◤		DMC-720	orange spice - dk
@		DMC-742	tangerine - lt
♣		DMC-895	hunter green - vy dk
▯		DMC-3348	yellow green - lt
◨		DMC-3362	pine green - dk
♪		DMC-3705	melon - dk
○		DMC-3727	antique mauve - lt
⌘		DMC-3805	cyclamen pink
✱		DMC-3837	lavender - ul dk
✖		DMC-3851	bright green - lt

10
20
30
40
50
70
80
90
100
110
10
20
30
40
50
60
70
80
90
100
110
120
130
140
150

Legend:

✖	DMC-21	alizarin - lt
◤	DMC-209	lavender - dk
◆	DMC-307	lemon
⌘	DMC-327	violet - dk
↑	DMC-502	blue green
◣	DMC-720	orange spice - dk
⊠	DMC-727	topaz - vy lt
▣	DMC-728	golden yellow
●	DMC-742	tangerine - lt
Ⓐ	DMC-761	salmon - lt
◆	DMC-817	coral red - vy dk
⊠	DMC-834	golden olive - vy lt
♣	DMC-904	parrot green - vy dk
◆	DMC-905	parrot green - dk
⋈	DMC-906	parrot green - md
◼	DMC-934	black avocado green
⊛	DMC-3722	shell pink - md
⬒	DMC-3801	christmas red - lt
✳	DMC-3851	bright green - lt

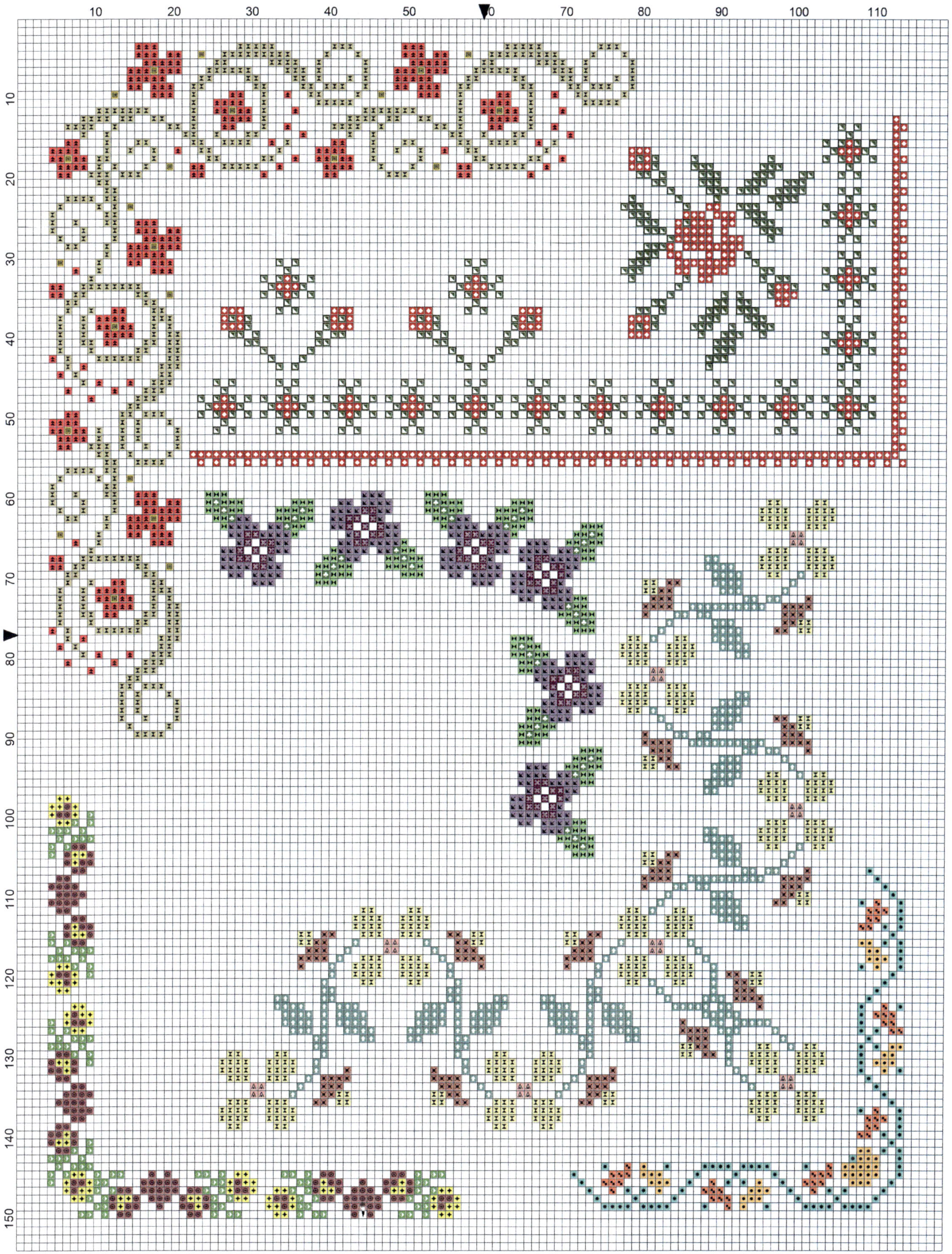

Legend:
- ◤ ▨ DMC-209　lavender - dk
- ◐ ▨ DMC-309　rose - dp
- ◆ ▨ DMC-817　coral red - vy dk
- ◧ ▨ DMC-906　parrot green - md
- ◣ ▨ DMC-986　forest green - vy dk
- ⌘ ▨ DMC-3805　cyclamen pink

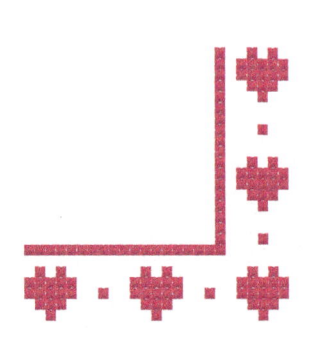

12

Legend:
- • DMC-209 lavender - dk
- ▲ DMC-327 violet - dk
- ♥ DMC-351 coral
- ⋈ DMC-444 lemon - dk
- ✖ DMC-501 blue green - dk
- ✚ DMC-740 tangerine
- ♣ DMC-895 hunter green - vy dk
- ⌶ DMC-906 parrot green - md
- ◐ DMC-917 plum - md
- ▣ DMC-3362 pine green - dk

13

10 20 30 40 50 60 70 80 90 100 110
10 20 30 40 50 60 70 80 90 100 110 120 130 140 150

Legend:
- ◐ ▨ DMC-351 coral
- ♣ ▨ DMC-501 blue green - dk
- ♥ ▨ DMC-817 coral red - vy dk
- • ▨ DMC-986 forest green - vy dk

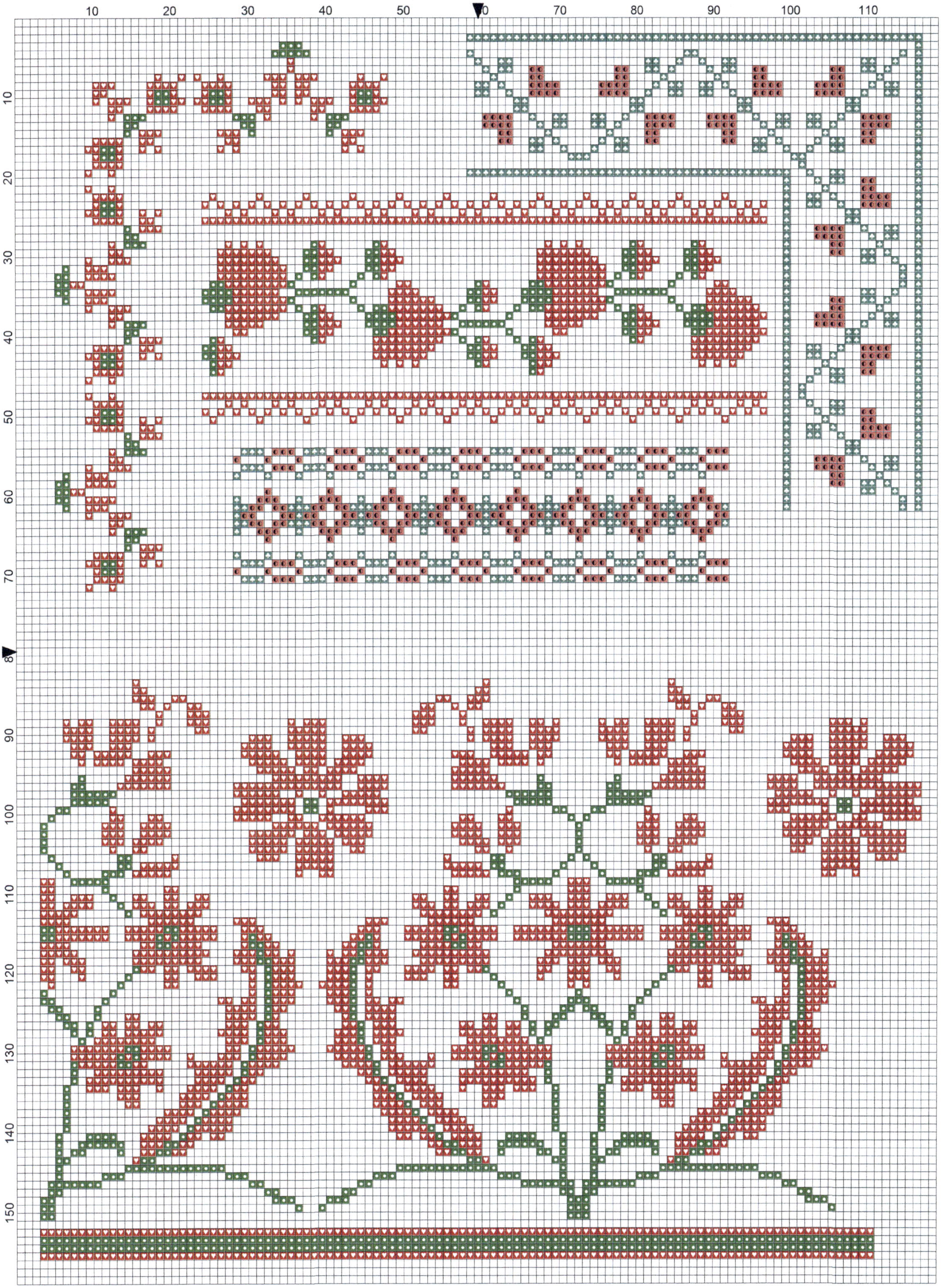

Legend:
- ♥ ■ DMC-321 christmas red
- ⌘ ■ DMC-351 coral
- ♣ ■ DMC-501 blue green - dk

10 20 30 40 50 60 70 80 90 100 110
10 20 30 40 50 60 70 80 90 100 110 120 130 140 150

Legend:

◣	■	DMC-9	cocoa - vy dk	♣	■	DMC-470	avocado green - lt
⋈	■	DMC-33	fuschia	⦵	■	DMC-898	coffee brown - vy dk
♥	■	DMC-321	christmas red	■	■	DMC-900	burnt orange - dk
✚	■	DMC-327	violet - dk	▲	■	DMC-906	parrot green - md
⌘	■	DMC-356	terra cotta - md	☒	■	DMC-3801	christmas red - lt

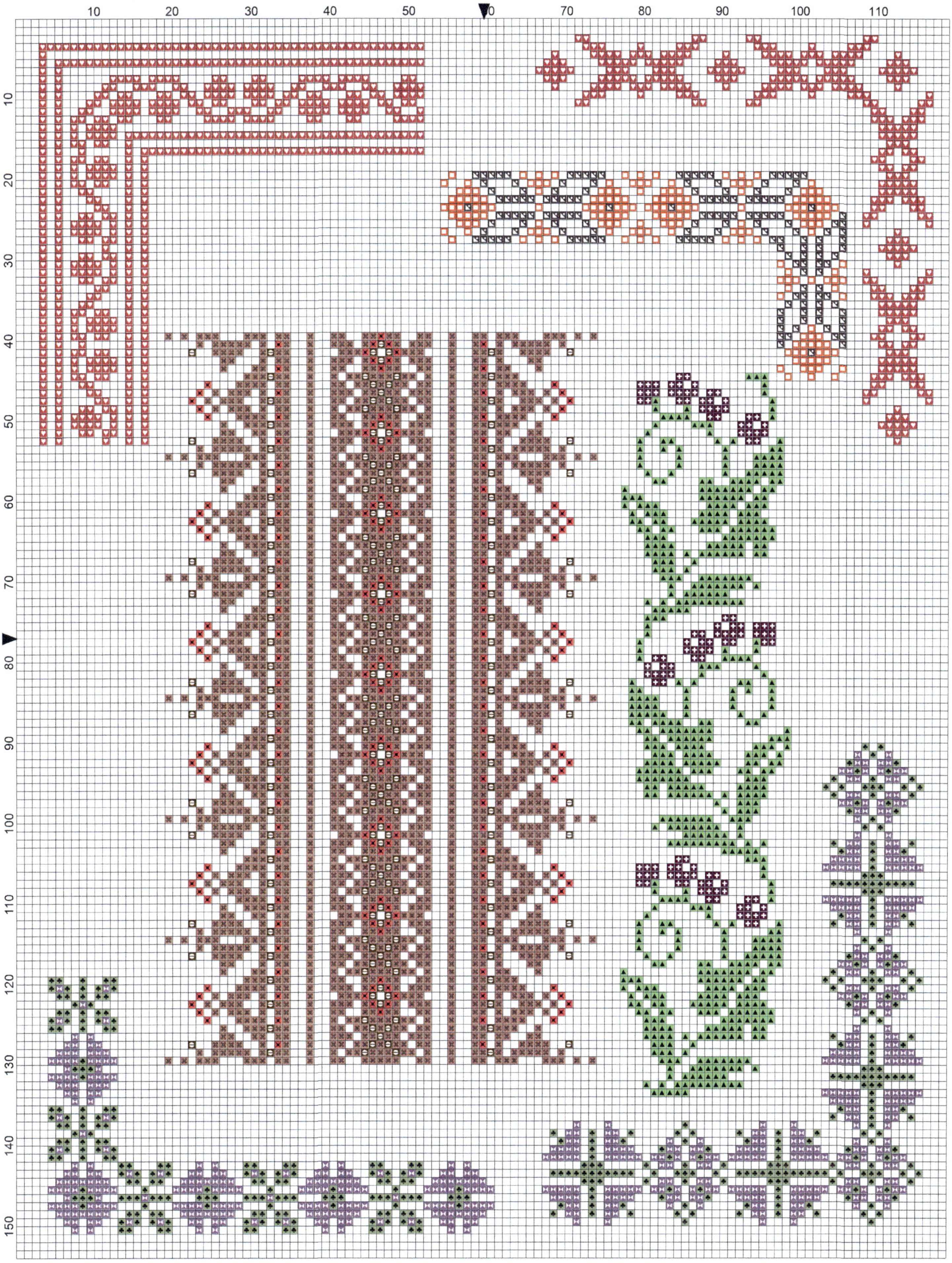

Legend:

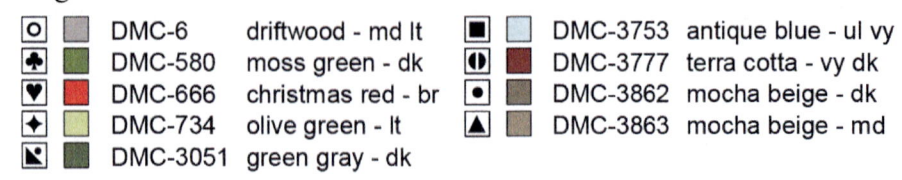

○	DMC-6	driftwood - md lt	■	DMC-3753	antique blue - ul vy
♣	DMC-580	moss green - dk	◐	DMC-3777	terra cotta - vy dk
♥	DMC-666	christmas red - br	●	DMC-3862	mocha beige - dk
♦	DMC-734	olive green - lt	▲	DMC-3863	mocha beige - md
◣	DMC-3051	green gray - dk			

22

Legend:

●	■	DMC-310	black
♣	■	DMC-580	moss green - dk
✦	■	DMC-734	olive green - lt
⊖	■	DMC-798	delft blue - dk
◆	■	DMC-996	electric blue - md
⤊	■	DMC-3777	terra cotta - vy dk
▲	■	DMC-3839	lavender blue - md

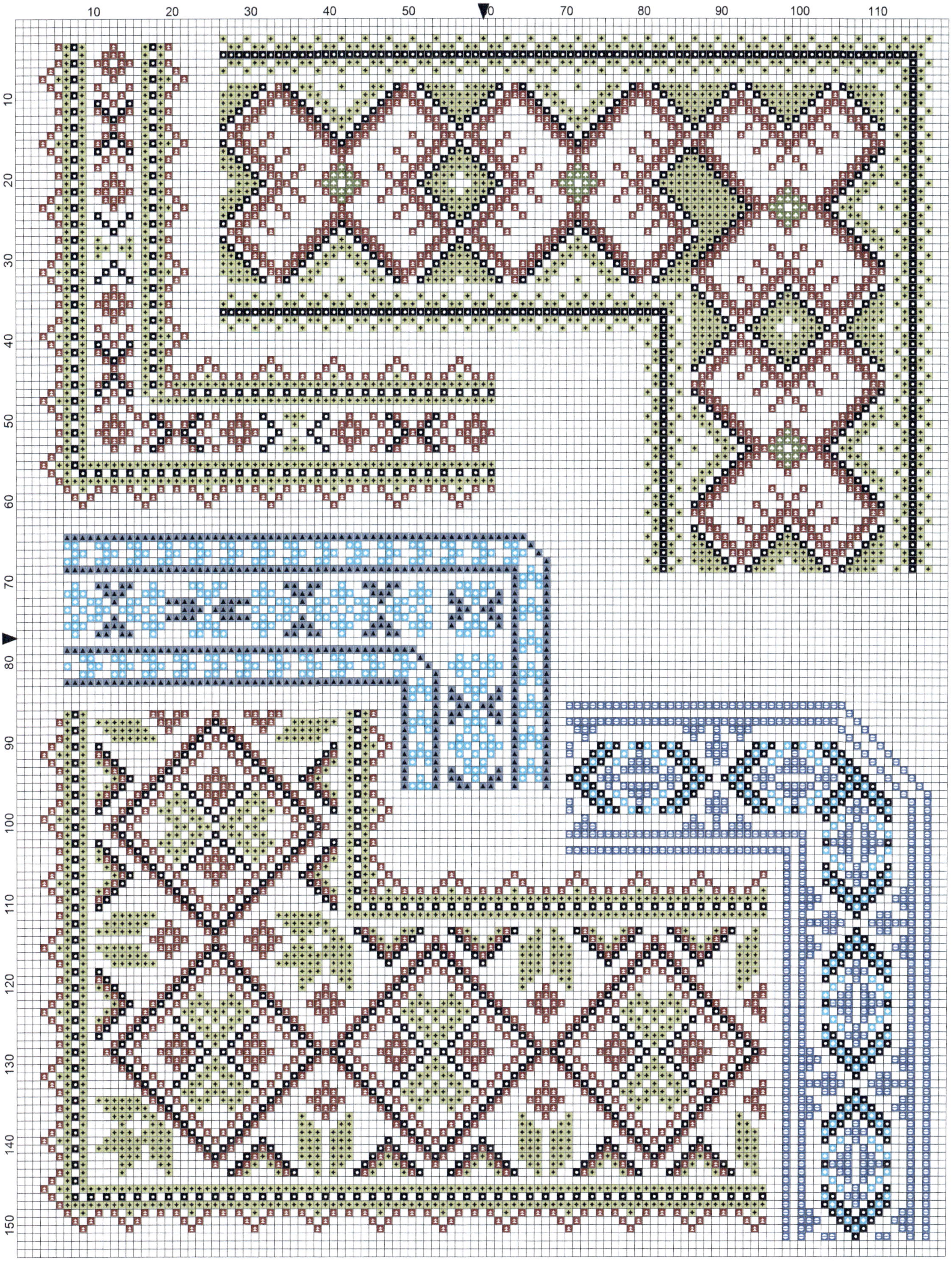

Legend:
- • ■ DMC-310 black
- ★ ▨ DMC-445 lemon - lt
- ✚ ▨ DMC-959 seagreen - md
- ◆ ▨ DMC-3747 blue violet - vy lt
- ✱ ▨ DMC-3787 brown gray - dk
- ♥ ▨ DMC-3801 christmas red - lt
- ♪ ▨ DMC-3839 lavender blue - md
- ◣ ▨ DMC-3842 wedgewood - vy dk
- ♣ ▨ DMC-3848 teal green - md
- ✖ ▨ DMC-3856 mahogany - ul vy lt

10 20 30 40 50 60 70 80 90 100 110
10 20 30 40 50 60 70 80 90 100 110 120 130 140 150

Legend:
- ● ■ DMC-310 black
- ★ ▢ DMC-445 lemon - lt
- ✱ ▢ DMC-728 golden yellow
- ♥ ▢ DMC-891 carnation - dk
- ♣ ▢ DMC-934 black avocado green
- ◐ ▢ DMC-959 seagreen - md
- ✖ ▢ DMC-3011 khaki green - dk
- ◤ ▢ DMC-3842 wedgewood - vy dk
- ▲ ▢ DMC-3848 teal green - md
- ⌘ ▢ DMC-3856 mahogany - ul vy lt

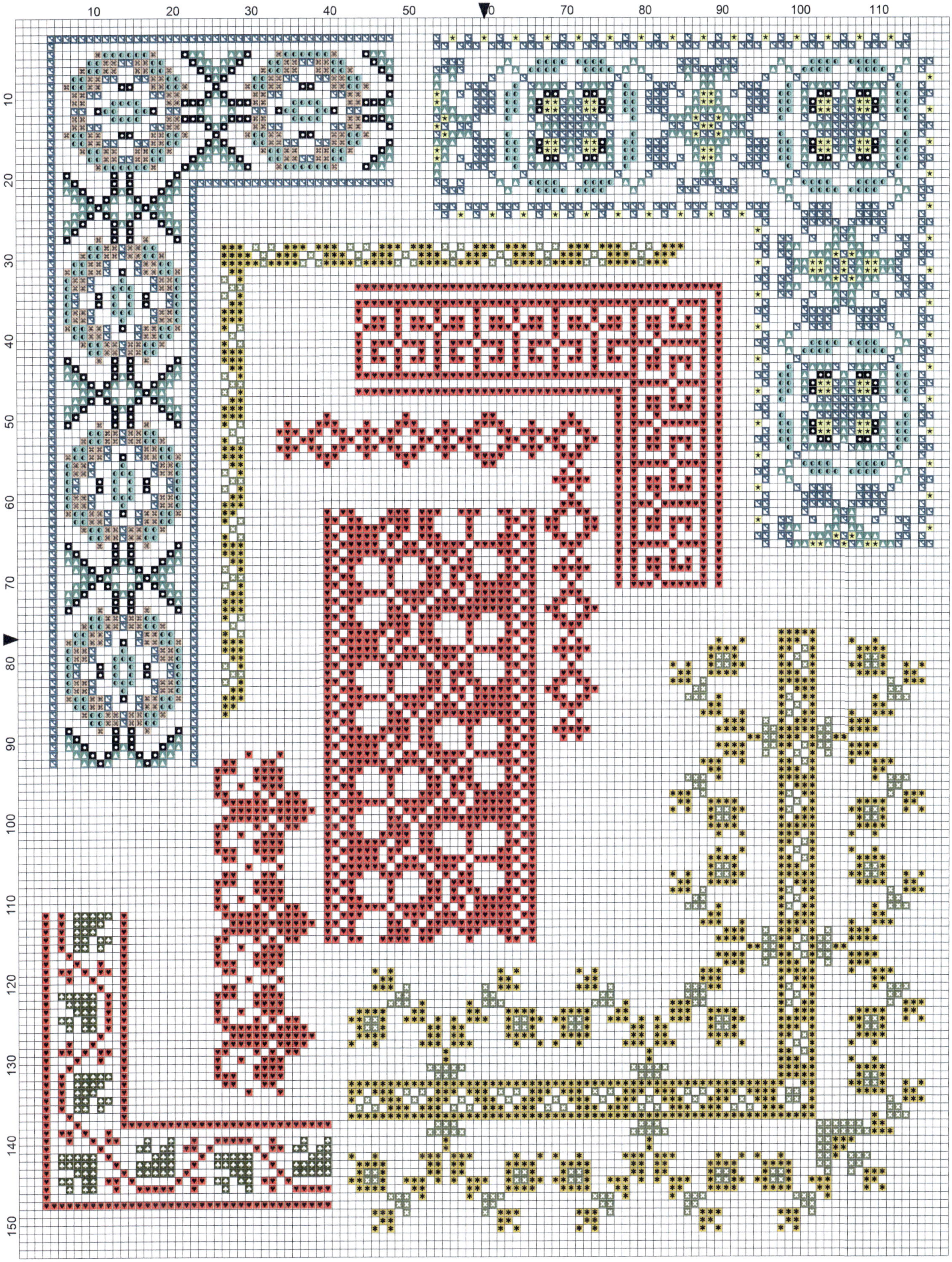

Legend:
- ● ■ DMC-317　pewter gray
- ♥ ■ DMC-720　orange spice - dk
- ✦ ■ DMC-964　seagreen - lt

10
20
30
40
50
60
70
80
90
100
110
10
20
30
40
50
60
70
80
90
100
110
120
130
140
150

Legend:
- ▲ DMC-728 golden yellow
- ♥ DMC-891 carnation - dk
- ♣ DMC-934 black avocado green
- ✚ DMC-3011 khaki green - dk

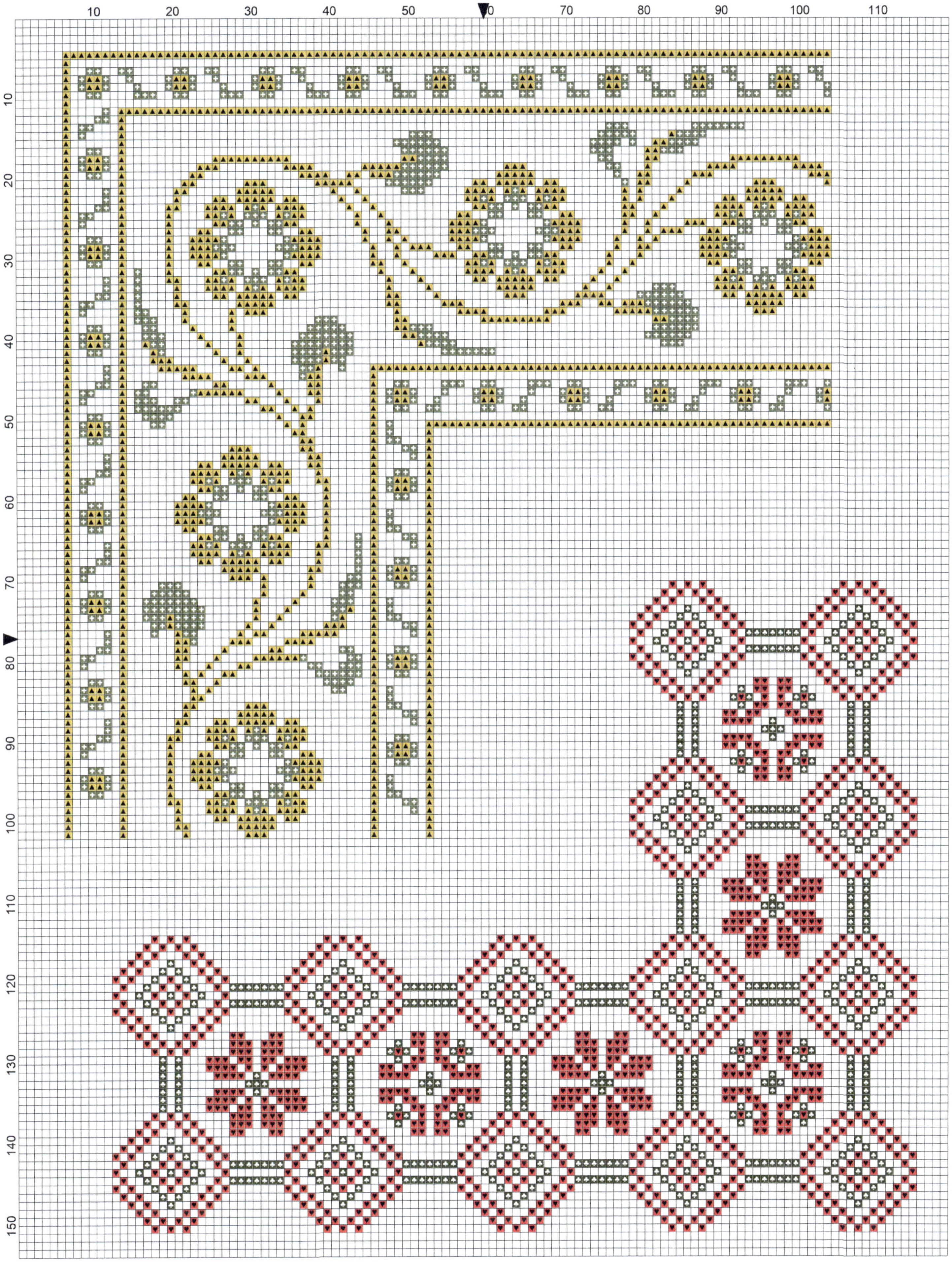

Legend:
- ♥ DMC-891 carnation - dk
- ♦ DMC-917 plum - md
- ♣ DMC-934 black avocado green
- ✚ DMC-3362 pine green - dk

10 20 30 40 50 60 70 80 90 100 110
10 20 30 40 50 60 70 80 90 100 110 120 130 140 150

Legend:
- ♥ DMC-817 coral red - vy dk
- ♦ DMC-891 carnation - dk
- ■ DMC-977 golden brown - lt
- ♣ DMC-986 forest green - vy dk
- ▲ DMC-3345 hunter green - dk
- ★ DMC-3881 avocado green - pl

36

Legend:
- ♣ DMC-502 blue green
- ✚ DMC-761 salmon - lt
- ♥ DMC-891 carnation - dk
- ✱ DMC-3345 hunter green - dk

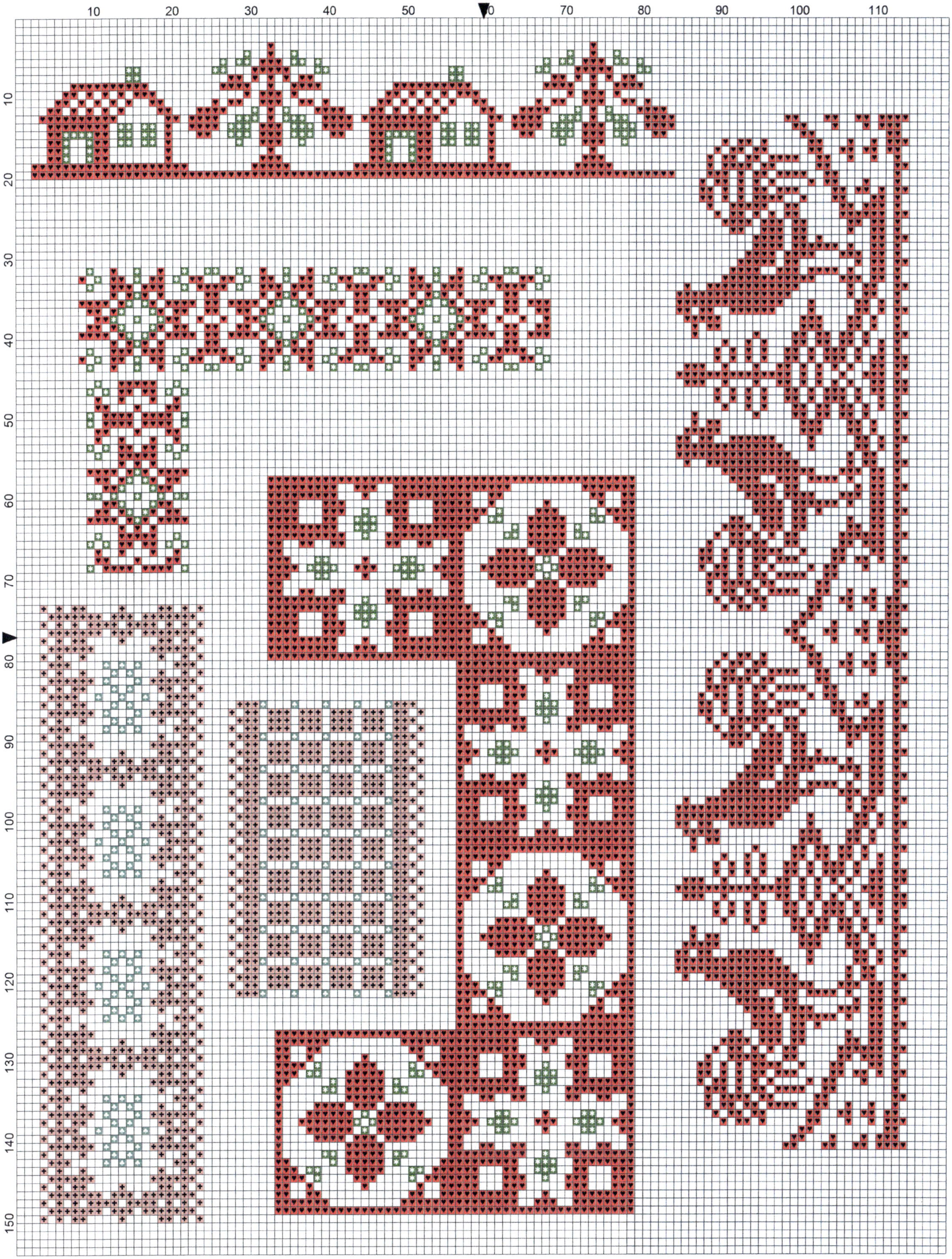
10
20
30
40
50
60
70
80
90
100
110
120
130
140
150

Legend:
- ♣ DMC-502 blue green
- ✱ DMC-701 christmas green - lt
- ♦ DMC-761 salmon - lt
- ♥ DMC-891 carnation - dk
- ▲ DMC-934 black avocado green
- ★ DMC-3722 shell pink - md

40

Legend:
- ⊡ ■ DMC-934 black avocado green
- ▲ ▨ DMC-3722 shell pink - md

42

Legend:

★		DMC-727	topaz - vy lt
♥		DMC-918	red copper - dk
■		DMC-922	copper - lt
♣		DMC-934	black avocado green
▲		DMC-3722	shell pink - md

44

Legend:
- ● ▢ DMC-318   steel gray - lt
- ♥ ▢ DMC-608   bright orange
- ▲ ▢ DMC-891   carnation - dk
- ✖ ▢ DMC-902   garnet - vy dk
- ★ ▢ DMC-922   copper - lt
- ⌘ ▢ DMC-958   seagreen - dk
- ◆ ▢ DMC-3768   gray green - dk

46

Legend:
- ● ▫ DMC-318 steel gray - lt
- ♥ ▫ DMC-608 bright orange
- ▲ ▫ DMC-891 carnation - dk
- ✖ ▫ DMC-902 garnet - vy dk
- ⌘ ▫ DMC-958 seagreen - dk
- ◆ ▫ DMC-3051 green gray - dk
- ▲ ▫ DMC-3768 gray green - dk

48

Legend:
- ● ▪ DMC-600 cranberry - vy dk
- ♥ ▪ DMC-891 carnation - dk
- ♣ ▪ DMC-895 hunter green - vy dk
- ⌘ ▪ DMC-3051 green gray - dk

10 20 30 40 50 60 70 80 90 100 110
10 20 30 40 50 60 70 80 90 100 110 120 130 140 150

Legend:
- ♥ DMC-600 cranberry - vy dk
- ♣ DMC-895 hunter green - vy dk
- ✖ DMC-3341 apricot
- • DMC-3371 black brown

10 20 30 40 50 70 80 90 100 110
10 20 30 40 50 60 70 80 90 100 110 120 130 140 150

Legend:
- ⊡ ■ DMC-413 pewter gray - dk

10 20 30 40 50 60 70 80 90 100 110
10 20 30 40 50 60 70 80 90 100 110 120 130 140 150

Legend:
- ● ■ DMC-9   cocoa - vy dk
- ✱ ■ DMC-601   cranberry - dk
- ★ ■ DMC-728   golden yellow
- ◆ ■ DMC-834   golden olive - vy lt
- ♣ ■ DMC-898   coffee brown - vy dk
- ♥ ■ DMC-3801   christmas red - lt

10 20 30 40 50 60 70 80 90 100 110
10 20 30 40 50 60 70 80 90 100 110 120 130 140 150

Legend:
- ● ■ DMC-9 cocoa - vy dk
- ★ ▢ DMC-307 lemon
- ♥ ▢ DMC-601 cranberry - dk
- ♣ ■ DMC-3750 antique blue - vy dk

58

Legend:
- ● DMC-9 cocoa - vy dk
- ▲ DMC-601 cranberry - dk
- ⊠ DMC-912 emerald green - lt
- ★ DMC-972 canary - dp
- ■ DMC-986 forest green - vy dk

10
20
30
40
50
70
80
90
100
110
10
20
30
40
50
60
70
80
90
100
110
120
130
140
150

Legend:
- ● ■ DMC-9 cocoa - vy dk
- ★ ■ DMC-307 lemon
- ✠ ■ DMC-601 cranberry - dk
- ✱ ■ DMC-912 emerald green - lt
- ◆ ■ DMC-972 canary - dp
- ♣ ■ DMC-986 forest green - vy dk
- ■ ■ DMC-3750 antique blue - vy dk

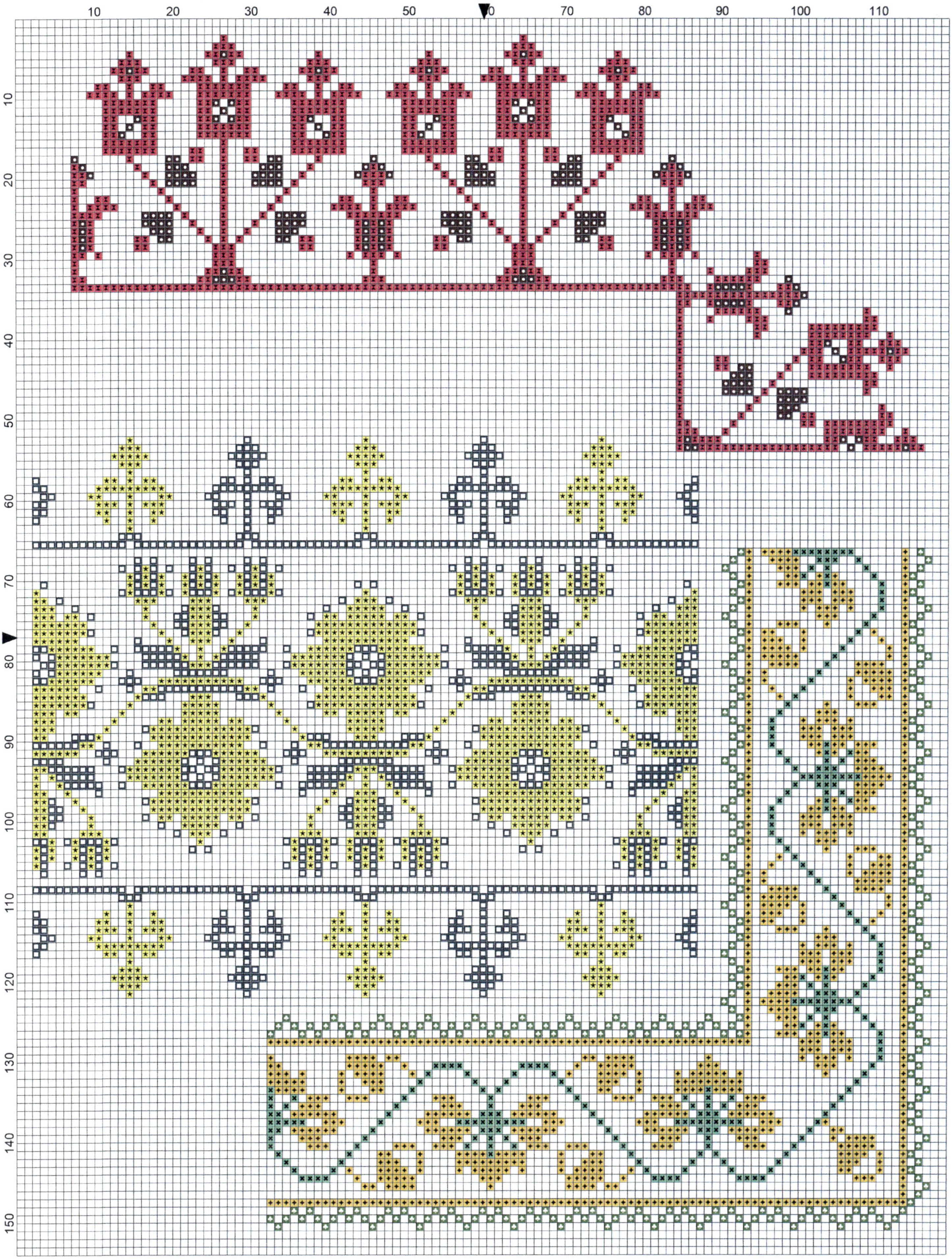

Legend:

●	■	DMC-9	cocoa - vy dk
✖	■	DMC-312	navy blue - lt
▲	■	DMC-319	pistachio green - vy dk
⋈	■	DMC-326	rose - vy dp
♥	■	DMC-601	cranberry - dk
✚	■	DMC-761	salmon - lt
⌘	■	DMC-813	blue - lt
◆	■	DMC-3843	electric blue

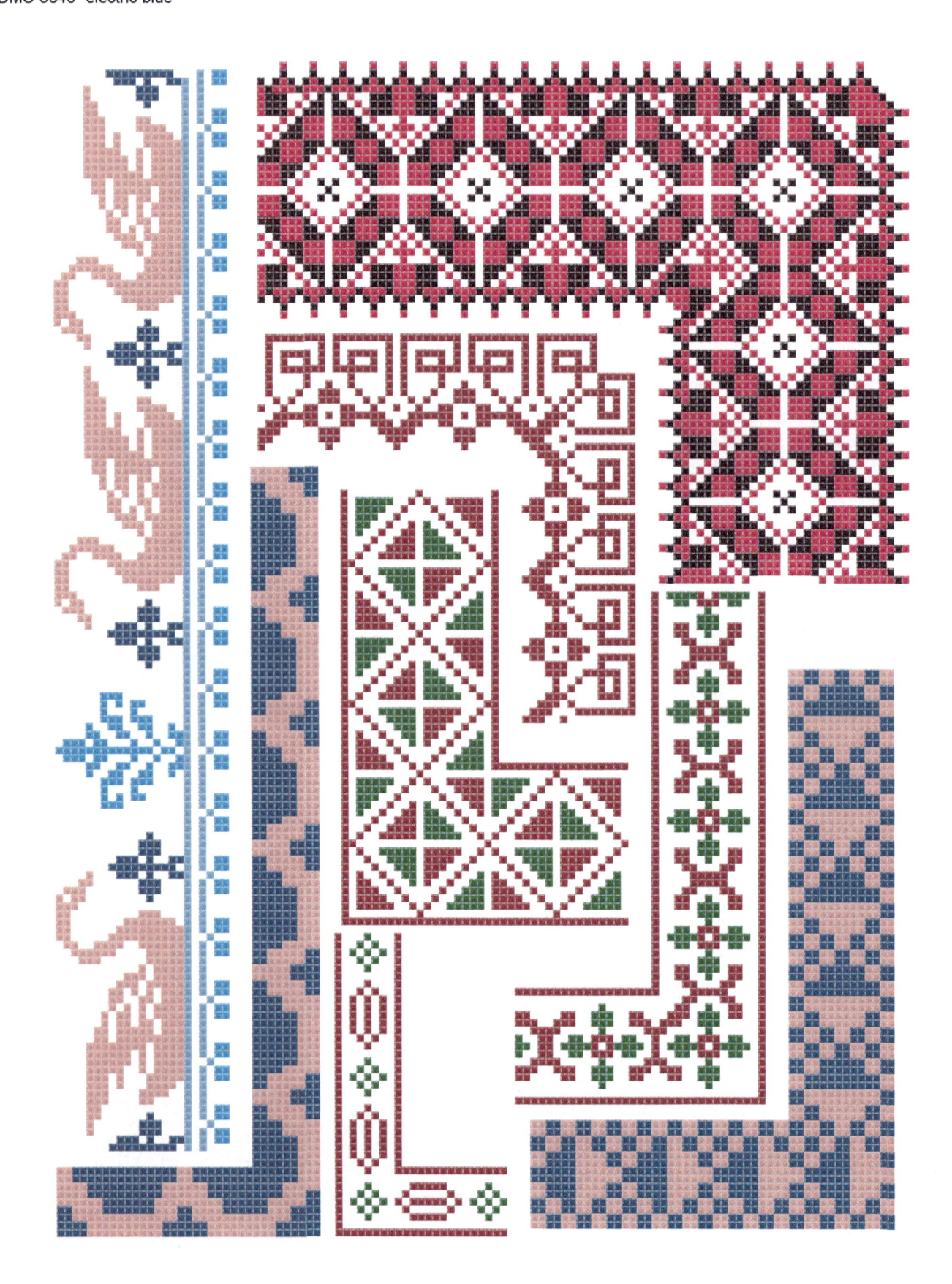

64

Legend:

★		DMC-12	tender green
■		DMC-13	nile green - md lt
♣		DMC-15	apple green
O		DMC-18	yellow plum
◆		DMC-316	antique mauve - md
▲		DMC-319	pistachio green - vy dk
✖		DMC-326	rose - vy dp
♥		DMC-351	coral
✱		DMC-603	cranberry
▲		DMC-3810	turquoise - dk
•		DMC-3840	lavender blue - lt

10 20 30 40 50 60 70 80 90 100 110
10 20 30 40 50 60 70 80 90 100 110 120 130 140 150

Legend:

- ▲ DMC-34   fuschia - dk
- ♥ DMC-349   coral - dk
- ● DMC-820   royal blue - vy dk
- ♦ DMC-839   beige brown - dk
- ♣ DMC-3347   yellow green - md
- ✉ DMC-3804   cyclamen pink - dk

10 20 30 40 50 60 70 80 90 100 110
10 20 30 40 50 60 70 80 90 100 110 120 130 140 150

Legend:

Symbol	Color	DMC	Name
✹		DMC-15	apple green
O		DMC-18	yellow plum
•		DMC-28	eggplant - md lt
⋈		DMC-221	shell pink - vy dk
♥		DMC-351	coral
■		DMC-813	blue - lt
✚		DMC-3024	brown gray - vy lt
⤊		DMC-3371	black brown
▲		DMC-3810	turquoise - dk

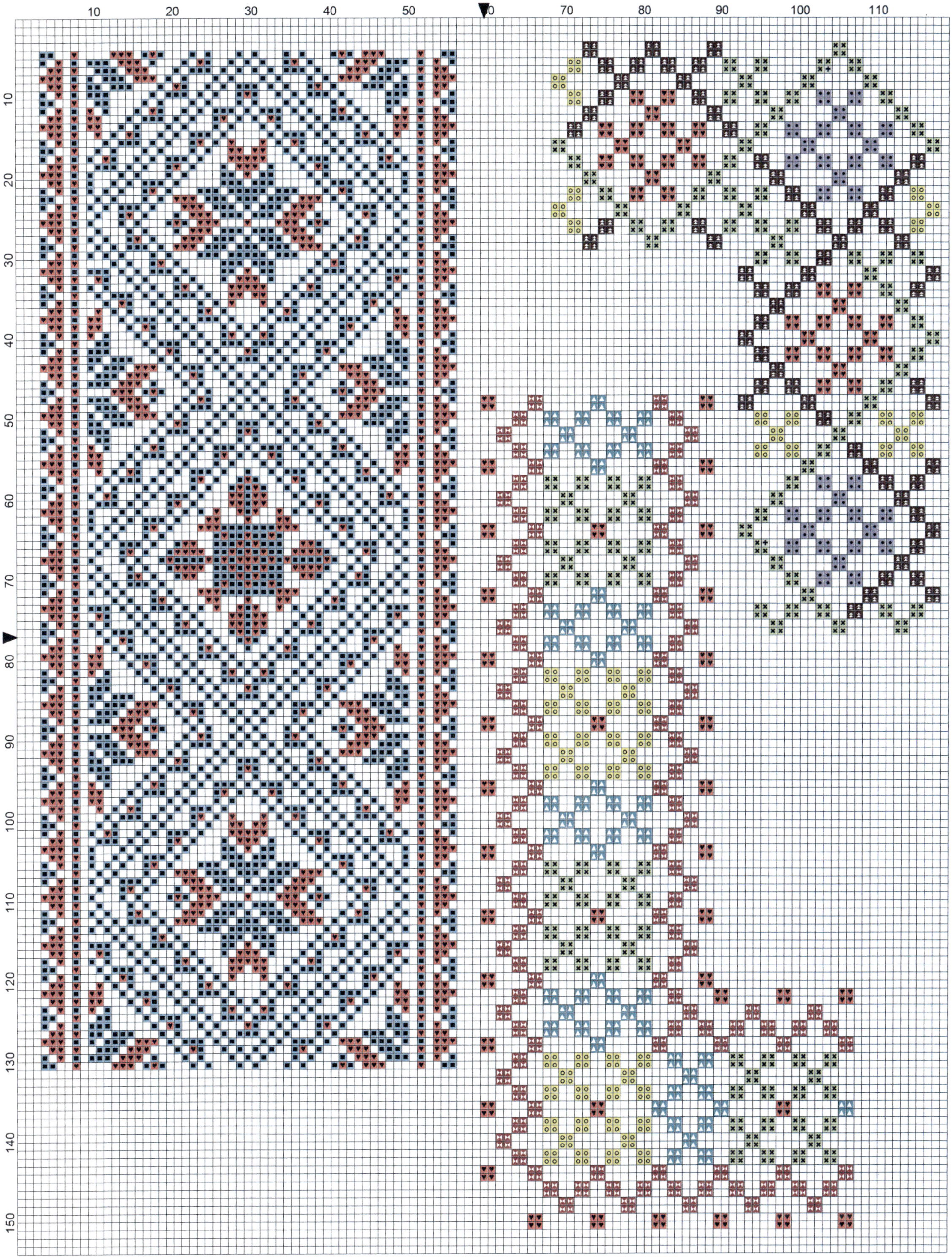

Legend:
- ✦ DMC-349 coral - dk
- • DMC-740 tangerine
- ✖ DMC-839 beige brown - dk
- ♥ DMC-917 plum - md

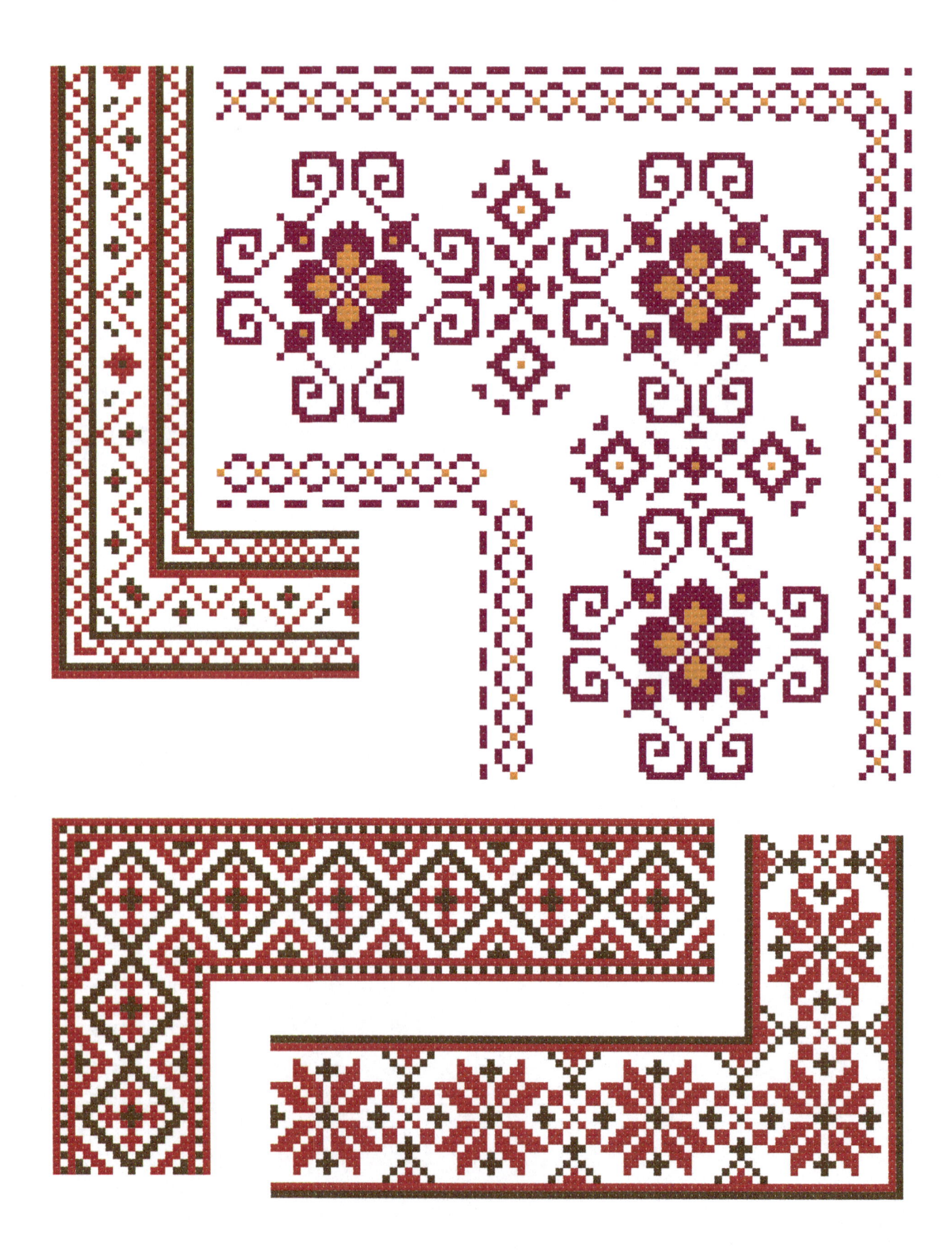

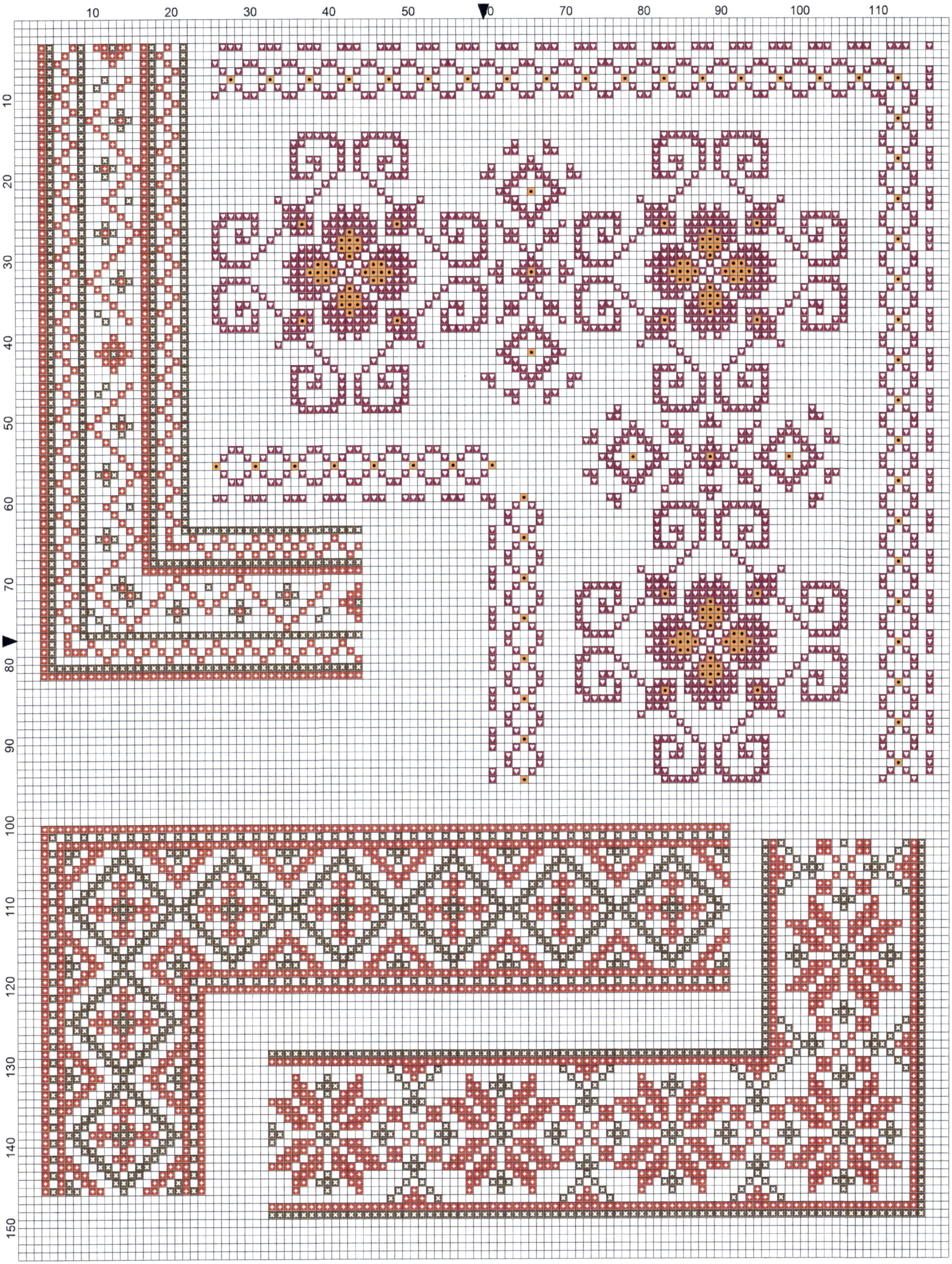

Legend:
- ♥ DMC-347 salmon - vy dk
- ● DMC-3021 brown gray - vy dk
- ✖ DMC-3341 apricot
- ▲ DMC-3607 plum - lt

74

Legend:

Symbol	Color	Code	Name
↑		DMC-13	nile green - md lt
•		DMC-310	black
◢		DMC-322	baby blue - dk
↙		DMC-335	rose
◣		DMC-415	pearl gray
↘		DMC-561	jade - vy dk
■		DMC-604	cranberry - lt
⌘		DMC-725	topaz
◆		DMC-817	coral red - vy dk
★		DMC-827	blue - vy lt
♣		DMC-911	emerald green - md
⋈		DMC-973	canary - br
◩		DMC-3371	black brown
▲		DMC-3801	christmas red - lt
◐		DMC-3843	electric blue
▣		DMC-3853	autumn gold - dk
✖		DMC-3882	cocoa - md lt
⇞		DMC-3890	turquoise - vy lt br

76

Legend:

Symbol	Color	Code	Name
◆		DMC-31	blueberry
⋈		DMC-704	chartreuse - br
▲		DMC-712	cream
L		DMC-776	pink - md
●		DMC-791	cornflower blue - vy dk
♣		DMC-989	forest green
✖		DMC-3608	plum - vy lt
★		DMC-3820	straw - dk

78

Choosing the right colors for your cross-stitch patterns can be tricky. But with our book 'Four Seasons Embroidery Color Palettes: 100 Embroidery Floss Color Charts',» it's easy! It's packed with seasonal colors and DMC floss codes, everything you need to make your designs pop. Forget sticking to pre-set pattern colors, let our palettes inspire you. With this book by your side, your embroidery work will always stand out!

Here are the links to grab your copy either as a paperback or for Kindle.

Kindle eBook: https://www.amazon.com/dp/B0C68GRB8W

Paperback: https://www.amazon.com/dp/B0C63YD96F

Alternatively, you can scan the QR code for quick access.

Kindle eBook

Paperback

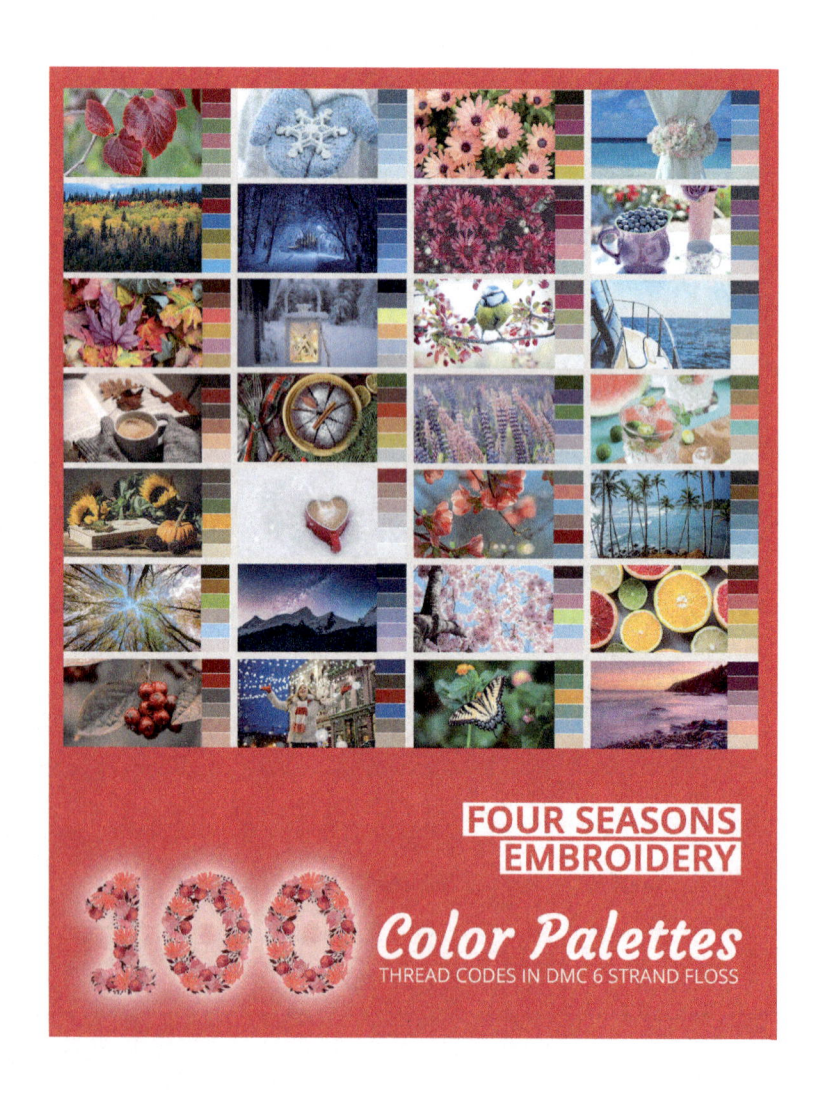

The written instructions, photographs, designs, patterns, and projects in this volume are intended for the personal use of the reader and may be reproduced for that purpose only. Any other use, especially commercial use, is forbidden under the law without the written permission of the copyright holder. Every effort has been made to ensure that all of the information in this book is accurate.

Printed in Great Britain
by Amazon